A RESOURCE FOR CHURCH

Inspirational Talks 2

'BEN' HUDDLESTON

Biblical quotations are taken from the Holy Bible, New
International Version, Copyright © 1973, 1978, 1984
International Bible Society, used by permission of
Zondervan Bible Publishers

Published in 2018 by Verité CM Ltd for 'Ben' Huddleston

British Library Cataloguing Data
A catalogue record of this book is available from
The British Library

Cover design, typesetting and production management by
Verité CM Ltd, Worthing, West Sussex UK
+44 (0) 1903 241975

Printed in England

Introduction

A useful resource for Ministers, Lay-Preachers and Group Leaders, giving seventeen 15-30 minute prepared talks, suitable for any occasion requiring a Bible-based inspirational talk.

Your own talk can be put together using the 'Outline'. Alternatively the complete 'Prepared Talk' can be used adding your own stories/thoughts where appropriate.

The talks can be adjusted to suit any age group or time slot. They are ideal for Services, Women's Meetings, Fellowship Groups, Home Groups, Lunch Clubs, Youth Clubs etc.

They are topical, practical, challenging and easy to use, and are particularly helpful if you need ideas and your preparation time is limited.

Dedication

This book is dedicated to the memory
of my beloved Aunt

Ruth Webley-Brooks

A true Woman of Faith!

Contents

Special Days

Time and Diaries

Subject: How we use and plan our time

Bible References: Psalm 90 verse 12

                            Psalm 139 verse 16

Visual Aid: A diary with pages full of appointments etc.

Outline:

1. Talk about how we fill our diaries and plan our days.

   Hold up current Diary showing pages full of activities.

2. The pace of modern life seems to dictate that we must be active and busy.

3. Are we enjoying our journey through life or are the days, weeks and years just flashing by because we are too busy?

4. What about God's plan for our lives – do we have time to find out what it is?

5. How much time do we set aside each day for God – to pray and read the Bible?

6. God is far more concerned about what we ARE than what we DO.

7. We each have an allotted time on this earth. We need to spend it wisely. We will have to account for what we have done for Jesus!

Prepared Talk

How many of us have one of these? (Hold up Diary) It used to be that we would carry a small diary in our handbags or pockets. Very often they were only used to record Birthdays we wanted to remember, or dates we needed reminding of such as the Dentist, Doctor, Hospital, Hairdresser; but now – these are what most of us seem to live by! Whether it's in this format or on our smartphone or ipad – our time is allocated to all sorts of activities and is booked up way ahead.

The Bible has a lot to say about 'time' and our use of it. We should never be so busy that we have only a little time spare for God or others who may need us. When did you last have a day with absolutely nothing at all planned or to do?

These days it seems we have been fooled into thinking that if we're not busy and doing things or going places; achieving recognition in some way or another for what we do, we're somehow missing out. If we don't conform to the general trends of life in the fast lane – we are told to 'get a life'!

But God has plans and a purpose for each of our lives, the trouble is many of us, both young and old are never still for long enough to find out what they are. Not one of us is on this earth by accident, our lives were planned by God before we were even conceived!

But are you really enjoying your journey through life? or is it just hard work and a drag and we're always looking ahead planning and filling our diaries with activities hoping for something better, rather than enjoying each day we are given?

What place does God have in your life? Is He included in your life at all? How often do you sit and talk to God in prayer; or is that left for emergencies only? Do you really know what's in this book – the greatest book ever written?

God will never force Himself on us. He quietly waits for us to 'get out of breath' with all our running around, and stop so that He can speak to us and we will hear His still small voice. It seems He sometimes allows things into our lives which cause us to have to stop and rest, and to slow the 'pace' down, so that He can actually teach us something, or give us what He wants us to do. It's a pity that we don't plan our lives to include more time to listen to Him!

When it comes to these things (diaries) we are all very organised. We are always thinking and planning ahead and setting time aside for holidays, events, celebrations, meetings, visiting friends and family etc., but how many of us have time set aside for God each day? I suspect we fill these up without thinking about that.

How important is it for us to spend time with Him? Since prayer is the powerhouse of our Christian lives, It is very important to take time to pray regularly. When was the last time we spent an hour talking to God? For sure there are enough needs and matters to pray about in life to spend half a day in prayer and still not cover everything!

 We think nothing of spending an hour on the phone to a friend or family member telling them all our troubles – yet what do we really achieve – nothing very often, because they don't have answers for us – but God does! There is a good little saying we may want to remember – 'Ask God for directions because He knows the way!'

When did we last spend an hour reading the Bible? We think nothing at all about spending several hours reading a novel or the newspaper, or watching TV. Now there's nothing wrong with any of those activities, but they don't feed our minds with wholesome and encouraging things, which will help us to live right; to love God and each other more; and to be using our time wisely.

In spite of all of our running around doing good things for folks, and working in the Church, attending meetings etc. God is far more interested in what we **ARE** than what we **DO**, because who we really are doesn't come from what we do in God's eyes; it's our relationship with Him that makes us what we should be and directs our thoughts and actions for Him.

How can we know what God wants for us and how to spend our time well? – by talking to Him in prayer and asking Him to show us what He wants us to do; and by reading the Bible and getting to know Him better. The way He guides us can be through circumstances; something someone says to us; something we read or come across in our daily living – He is a practical God and knows what we need.

All around us these days people are making a name for themselves by what they do and we all praise them and hold them in high regard, because in the world today we are measured by our achievements. But God sees us differently from the way others see us – He sees right into our hearts and knows our thoughts and motives and who we really are.

We each have an allotted time in this life – the length of which is known only to God. Psalm 139 says this – "All the days ordained for me were written in your book before one of them came to be". We've talked about time and the pace of our lives these days, but where does God feature in it all? That for all of us is an important question. We have been thinking about our use of time and in Psalm 90 we read this – verse 10 and 12. We need to remember that life here is limited, so we must use our time wisely, as one day we will account for it before God but He also wants us to enjoy our lives and all the blessings He has for us.

There are some amazing things in here planned for the future. Unlike our plans which may or may not come to pass – what's in here really will happen because this contains God's Word and His word is true; it contains His promises – and they are never broken; it contains His plans for mankind and they will happen!

The one event we all need to be planning for is the return of Jesus. "But we don't know when it will be, so how can we plan for it" people ask. The Bible tells us two things about Jesus coming back again, which will help (1) It will happen suddenly and when we don't expect it! and (2) there will be unusual things happening in our world (which are mentioned in the Bible) when it is very near!

This is a controversial subject in many ways, as people don't really want to think too much about it. We are so busy and settled in our lives here; and in many churches it is not talked about, but we only have to read our Bible and we will see very clearly that it's a date in God's diary that is getting closer! Many a time people will dismiss the subject, and say "Oh don't worry about that, there's a lot to happen yet before Jesus returns!"

Some of the events pointing to the soon return of Jesus are beginning to happen in the world around us right now, and we need to be thinking much more about what all of this means for us and our lives as Christians or otherwise!

So if Jesus is going to return soon, what do we need to do:

Firstly, be ready ourselves by being sure we know and belong to Him. How can we be sure about that – Romans 10 says this (verses 9-11).

Secondly, we need to be telling others about God's love for them – they need to know. As Christians, we need to be spending more time letting our loved ones and family who are not believers, know about Jesus. We need to be bold and courageous and not be worried about what they will think of us! It truly is a matter of life and death for them!

Thirdly, Read the Bible and learn what signs to watch out for in the days leading up to Jesus' return – many are happening right now before our eyes!

It makes very interesting and exciting reading and there are many books to help us understand what the Bible is saying.

Verse 12 in Psalm 90 says we should ask the Lord to teach us how to use our time on this earth wisely, not to waste it on trivialities, so that we will be wise and understand the things concerning our spiritual wellbeing, and therefore be able to tell others about Him.

We cannot stop the passage of time! But we can put our time to better use; and we can be prepared ourselves for His return, and also prepare the hearts of others to receive Him before it's too late.

Perhaps we should write in our diaries each morning: 'Will He come today!'

That way we may live a bit differently!

Relating to Others

Subject: Our 'people skills' are affected by the way we see ourselves.

Do we consider ourselves better than others? Are we likeable?

Are people 'drawn' to us or do they avoid us? As Christian people it is important how we relate to others.

Bible References: Proverbs 11 verses 13, 16 and 25

Proverbs 15 verse 30

Proverbs 17 verse 17

Proverbs 18 verse 13

Ephesians 4 verse 2

Philippians 4 verse 8

Outline:

1. How do we really see ourselves?

2. How we see ourselves can affect our attitudes towards others.

3. We need to be honest with ourselves and others always.

4. Do we consider ourselves better than others?

5. How do we come across to people in reality – are we cheerful and approachable; are we 'known to moan' all the time; are we a talker and not a listener?

6. Looking at the Bible verses, how do we really measure up?

7. We all need to do a regular 'self-check'

8. Something to remember –'We need to be a friend to have a friend'!

9. The Bible says "A friend loves at all times" are we able to do that?

Prepared Talk:

How are your 'people skills' – to use a modern expression. In other words, how do we relate to others? How do you see yourself. For sure it's probably not as others see you! How we see ourselves is actually quite important.

You may for example have a low opinion of yourself – possibly because you feel you've never succeeded at much in your life, and have regrets. It may be you simply didn't have the circumstances which offered you opportunity to do well academically or in other ways, and all your life you've been down on yourself. This can actually affect how you relate to other people.

For example, when someone pays you a compliment about how you look, or something you've done; how do you receive it? Do you say "Oh it's nothing" or "it wasn't very good really", or do you simply say "thank you". If you say anything other than "thanks", you may be throwing a kind gesture back at someone, and questioning their judgement. They probably won't bother paying you a compliment again!

If someone says something nice, not only is it meant to make us feel good about ourselves, but our response can make the other person feel they've done something nice too. We all need encouragement and building up!

When someone sees you coming into Church or you are standing at the front to read, lead or give notices; or if you stand at the door to greet people; or serve their tea and coffee; what do you suppose people are thinking as they observe your manner and attitude? When folks see you coming down the road towards them – what do you imagine they are thinking?

We would all like to think their reaction would be "Oh, here's Mary or Jack (or whatever your name is) how nice to see her/him, I'd like to have a chat"! Or might they be thinking "Oh,oh, here's so and so, with a face like someone sucking a lemon", "I'll pretend I'm in a hurry, otherwise I'll get the last 6 months medical history; or the latest gossip about who's said or done something wrong in the fellowship or village"! How awful to think that might be how people really see us!

On the other hand of course, it could be that you have too high an opinion of yourself. You may think that because you've had a reasonable education, a stable family life, a bit of money in the bank, a good career etc. that you are actually better than some people.

We have no right to think ourselves better that others. Two of Jesus' Disciples thought they were better than the others and asked for special positions in heaven, but Jesus told them, that in order to become great, they needed to become servants! The bible tells us we should consider others better than ourselves. That's not easy to do usually, because pride comes into it!

When we call ourselves Christians, we are identifying with the name of Christ, therefore we need to reflect Him in our daily living. If we profess to be Christians, we will be under observation from people around us. If we don't apply the teachings of Jesus to the way we behave and relate to others, then we are simply pretending. Real Christianity should cause us to think of others first and be careful how we treat people.

A few tips from the Bible about how we can become a better friend to others:

Don't Gossip   Proverbs 11 verse 13 and Proverbs 17 verse 9

Be Cheerful   Proverbs 15 verse 30

Be Kind   Proverbs 11 verse 16

Be Generous   Proverbs 11 verse 25

Be Humble   Ephesians 4 verse 2

Be a listener   Proverbs 18 verse 13

Having looked at what the Bible says about how we should treat others – how do we measure up? We need to be honest, as God sees our hearts and knows things that others don't!

We may feel we can't live up to God's standards, but He's there to help us and loves us whatever, and we must in turn love others.

Counterfeit

Subject: Discerning between genuine and 'counterfeit' Christianity

Bible References: Romans 3 verse 23

John 3 verse 16

Visual Aid: a piece of valuable jewellery or a valuable item – and an item that looks similar but is really worth little or nothing – a copy or fake. (China, coins, perfume, clothing would be suitable examples)

Outline:

1. Talk about programmes on TV such as Antiques Roadshow or Fake Britain.

2. Use something as a visual aid which is valuable, and something similar which is a fake or copy.

3. Many people are out to fool or deceive us today – give examples.

4. Use illustration of famous 'Footballer' Carlos Kaiser, who conned everyone for years into believing he was a great footballer and lived a luxurious life to match, but never played a game!

5. There are many people around today who believe and can give the impression that they are real Christians, yet in reality do not have a genuine relationship with God – are not 'born again' as Jesus said we must be. (Story of Nicodemas).

6. The Bible makes it clear that no one is sinless, we are all in need of forgiveness. (Romans 3 verse 23)

7. It's important to make sure we understand what a true Christian is.

8. It will matter at the end of this life!

Prepared Talk

Many folks enjoy watching television programmes about antiques and collectable items, where people bring along their prized possessions and things they have inherited, to get a valuation as to what they are really worth. Some folks bring beautiful items which are valued at very little and some bring ordinary things that turn out to be worth tens of thousands of pounds.

A lady and gentleman on one such programme brought along a bag they saw in a skip, which contained bits and pieces of jewellery, only to find that it was actually full of exquisite items of ruby and emerald jewellery worth around £40,000! But sadly that's a rare occurrence. Many bring along things they've inherited, believing them to be priceless, only to be told they are counterfeit!

A few years ago, there were around 30 million counterfeit £1 coins in circulation. People were told how to identify them, and if they had any should take them to the Bank as they were not legal tender.

Many searched through their money boxes and purses and came across a number of counterfeit £1 coins, but it was hard to spot them, because they were so cleverly done and so close to the original. Most people of course had no idea they were using counterfeit coins.

There are many dishonest people out in the world today who are out to fool us and to deceive us in all kinds of ways. You can go to an ordinary market and pick up a real bargain with a well-known store name on it or makers tag, only to find later on that it falls apart or breaks down because it's not the real thing, and therefore doesn't carry a guarantee if it goes wrong. It is very difficult to know what is genuine these days.

Use Visual Aid at this point.

So how can we tell what's real and what's counterfeit? Well, it's pretty difficult and often takes an expert in the field to tell us how to spot something that's not genuine, and that includes people!

There are shopping channels on the TV and they sell the most exquisite jewellery. Some of what they sell are copies of real diamonds, and they are beautiful. It's easy to see how people can be completely fooled into thinking they are genuine. One Presenter told the story of a lady who had brought one of the imitation diamond rings, but set in Gold. She had taken it to a high street jeweller for valuation, and for a few seconds, the Jeweller was almost fooled into thinking they were real diamonds!

We are talking about counterfeits and things that we may think are real when they are not, because it's possible that the same thing can occur in the Christian Church!,

There are many people who go to Church on a regular basis, and are actively involved in all the activities, including leadership, yet they are not 'real' Christians.

So what is meant by that – not a 'real' Christian?

The Bible tells us that to be a real Christian, we have to do something very definite.

To belong to God, it's not enough to go to Church regularly, live a 'good' life, help others, give to charity and so on, or even be Baptised and think that makes us Christians. The Bible tells us it is more than just those things.

None of us like to think we are not good – but we all sin. This is because of what happened in the Garden of Eden, when Adam and Eve sinned against God, and as a result everyone born after that has a sinful nature. Because of that God sent Jesus, to teach and show us how to live, and He eventually gave His life and took the punishment that we were due, in His own body on the cross.

When we accept that He did it for us as individuals, then we need to ask His forgiveness for our sin and allow His Holy Spirit to live within us, in other words we start over (are 'born again' as the Bible describes it) – that's what make us 'real' Christians. We have to make that decision and commitment.

You see, there is only one who can possibly know for sure whether we are truly Christians and that is God Himself. No-one can see into our heart except Him. No-one knows your thoughts except you and Him.

Now you may think "so what" as long as people around me think I'm kind and nice and a good person it doesn't matter. It actually matters a great deal to God!

It is quite possible to fool people around us into thinking we are Christians, but God you cannot fool, and one day we will all stand before Him, and it's at that time that He will separate out those who truly belong to Him and those who do not. Only those who are His will spend eternity with Him in heaven. Unlike the general thinking in the world today, not everyone is going to heaven when they die. The Bible is very clear about that.

If you are not 100% sure that you are a 'real' Christian and that you will be going to heaven when you die, then you should do something about it today.

It could be that you have attended Church or Chapel since you were a tiny child, and yet you have never taken that step of putting your trust and faith in Jesus. This is such an important matter.

We have talked today about 'counterfeit' – or things that look like the real thing, but really they are not. That could be applied to being a Christian too! It's all too easy to say and do the right things, and believe there is a God, but not have had a real change of heart.

Remember – God knows the real us!

Put on Love

Subject: Love is very important in life.

Where does it come from?

We are told we must put on, or clothe ourselves with love so that others can see it.

Bible References: Colossians 3 verses 12-14

Ephesians 6 verse 10

Outline:

1. What is love. Where does it come from?

2. Our hearts are the centre of love, the centre of our being – our soul, the part of us that relates to God.

3. We all need to love and be loved – love is shown in many different ways. Suggest and discuss ways of showing love to others.

4. Spiritual love – the love between God and us.

5. The Bible tells us to 'put on love', as we would put on a garment, to clothe ourselves with love.

6. Love in the Dictionary is described as being a strong feeling of affection, and that usually means we put others first, and are prepared to make sacrifices. Jesus did – because of Love for us.

Prepared Talk

Love is a very interesting thing. No one can define what it is. We know that it is a very powerful emotion, and plays a big part in all of our lives.

The Bible has a lot to say about it, and the heart is at the centre of our thinking about love.

So where does love come from? The simple answer to that is God! The Bible tells us God **is** Love. He is the very essence of love, it is His nature. In the 1970's everyone had little sayings beginning 'Love is…' and they all suggested the sort of things we would do to show love. For us, love begins in our hearts. So let's look at 'hearts' from God's perspective, because our heart is very different to the romantic little red shapes we see depicting love on cards etc.

The heart is referred to as the centre of our being – the soul of us – the real us.

The literal heart of course is a fleshy organ which pumps our blood around our bodies, and is vital to our existence because if it fails to work – it's curtains – as we say! The 'heart' of us that God refers to so much in His Word, is the part that makes us who we are, our person, our soul.

When we put our trust in God, we have a change of heart, and life takes on a different meaning. We look to the bible for help and guidance, and how God wants us to live our lives.

On a practical level, each year, as the weather starts to cool down at the end of the summer and into the Autumn, there are things which we need to 'put on' for our 'physical wellbeing'. We usually have to start around September by putting on a cardigan, then we add a jacket, then we get to the warm winter coats. We also have to put on scarves and hats and gloves. We have to swop our sandals and open shoes and put on sensible shoes and warm boots. All of this is to keep us warm and cosy and to protect us from the cold, this is particularly important as we get older!

There are other things also we have to 'put on' at this time of year – we put on our central heating or fires in the evenings when we sit down. We put on our lights much earlier since the clocks have changed, and we put on our winter duvet or extra blankets as well. All of these things are to keep us warm.

Now the Bible is a very practical and amazing book, and we are told that there are some things that we need to 'put on' this time for our 'spiritual wellbeing' and protection all year round – not just for a season.

You will probably be familiar with the verses in the bible that encourage us to 'put on' the whole armour of God. Now if you've ever been on a visit to Windsor Castle, there are whole areas set aside for suits of armour and weapons used to protect people in the event of a battle. They look incredibly heavy and cumbersome, and you wonder however men were able to stand up, let alone fight in them, but they had to be strong to protect them in the right way.

In Ephesians Chapter 6 and verse 10 we are told to **put on** our spiritual 'armour' because we are in a daily battle against evil. We need some protection and knowledge of how to withstand the attacks from Satan – who by the way is very real! So what armour must we put on and why?

The belt of truth: We must stand up for what we know to be True and live accordingly

The breastplate of Righteousness: In olden times when soldiers were going into battle, the solid breastplate kept them safe from being pierced by swords and spears into their hearts and vital organs.

We have to be able to withstand the attacks from Satan aimed at our hearts and minds by standing for justice and what is morally correct.

Shoes: We need to be prepared for our daily Christian walk, with our feet ready to go out and share the Gospel with others.

The Shield of Faith: That is to protect us from the 'arrows' or attacks that Satan will direct at us to try and undermine our trust in God. We need to rely on and remember what we have learned about God. "Never doubt in the darkness what you have learned in the light"!

Helmet of Salvation: The helmet not only protects but is a symbol of Victory over evil – in other words our hope in God.

The Sword of the Spirit: That is the Word of God – The Bible. We need to read and remember things from the Bible which we can call on to encourage us when we feel under attack or pressure from evil. (For example when someone is telling us that it's ok to do something that we know God has told us in the Bible is wrong, we can tell them it's wrong and stand against evil by quoting what the Bible says.)

All of those items are like our 'spiritual' clothing if you like, but those aren't the only things God tells us to 'put on'. This is what He says in Colossians Chapter 3 verses 12-14:

Put on:

Compassion:	Sympathy & pity or concern for others. Sometimes we get so caught up with our own problems and worries that we overlook the needs of others.

Kindness:	Being considerate and generous.
Humility:	Having a modest or low opinion of your own importance
Gentleness:	Being mild and kind – not harsh or severe
Patience:	Having the ability to accept delay, trouble or suffering without getting angry or upset.
Forgiveness:	An obvious and very important thing.

Last of all over all these virtues put on Love.

All through the Bible we read that Love is the most important thing of all – "the greatest of these is Love". Love in the Dictionary is described as being a strong feeling of affection, and that usually means we put others first, and are prepared to make sacrifices. Jesus did – because of His Love for us.

As we 'put on' our warmer clothes, in the winter months, remember the things God has told us to 'put on' for our spiritual protection, and things we should 'put on' or make sure we have as character traits.

If we are Christians and truly walking with the Lord then these are important lessons for us to take on board – no matter how long we have been Christians, there is always room for improvement!

So each day when you open your wardrobe and decide what to wear – remember to make sure that as you get dressed for the day, the last thing you 'put on' metaphorically speaking is Love. Ask the Lord as you get ready to face each day, to clothe you with love and you won't go far wrong!

The first thing that folks notice about us usually when they see us coming is what we're wearing – so let it be 'Love' – an attitude which will show in our faces and cheer others too!

It's all in the Small Print!

Subject: Insurance and Life Assurance both physical and Spiritual!

Bible Verses: Romans 10 verses 9,10 and 11

Outline:

1. Talk about insurances that most of us have for daily life, and Life Assurance for our families when we die.

2. All have terms and conditions – usually in small print and difficult to read and understand!

3. Terms and conditions are attached to most things as a safeguard against people defaulting on their contract.

4. We now have Health & Safety Regulations, the first rule of which is "We are responsible for our own safety"

5. How do these things relate to God and faith?
   We need both insurance and assurance for peace of mind.
   Insurance is a safeguard against loss or failure.
   Assurance is an insurance on our lives which guarantees a 'payout' on our death.

6. Explain God's conditions for our security for Eternity.

7. Have we read the 'small print' in the bible to know what God requires of us so that we can have peace of mind in this life and a secure future in Eternity.

Prepared Talk

Most of us have Insurances – health, home, car etc. Some of us have Life Assurance? Many also have bank accounts, credit cards etc.

What's the difference between Insurance and Assurance? Well, Insurance is a guarantee of financial compensation for loss, illness or death in return for payments made on a regular basis.

Life Assurance promises that money will be paid to named beneficiaries such as our children or spouse when the Insured person dies. It's all about having 'peace of mind' that our loved ones will be cared for when we have gone.

BUT – everything – insurance and assurance policies, bank accounts, credit cards, household service contracts etc. all come with 'terms and conditions' and those terms and conditions are usually copious lists and pages of hard to understand clauses, usually in very small print – many believe as a deterrent to stop us reading them so that we don't realise exactly what we get and don't get, that is promised when we're sold these commodities!

There are programmes on the television, such as 'Watchdog' and 'Rip-off Britain', where the presenter and researchers, uncover the reality of the things we sign up to, and more often than not they're not at all what we believe we have!

Why do we have all these terms and conditions anyway? Well, sadly because these days in particular, there seems to be a distinct lack of trust in the world, and companies providing these services have to cover themselves for every eventuality. For example, some folks will go and buy a household item like a washing machine or something, not read the manufacturer's instructions properly, misuse it, and damage or break it, and they then march back to the store demanding a refund or replacement all because they couldn't be bothered to read the 'small print' about proper use and their responsibility!

Our current society has a culture of suing, so that if you are to blame for anything which goes wrong, people can now take you to court and try to get compensation from you.

So what has all this about terms and conditions and insurance etc. got to do with God or our faith?

Well, most of us probably have insurances etc. to give us peace of mind in case things go wrong in life. But what about peace of mind over what happens when we die? It may be that some of us think that doesn't matter because we will all go to heaven anyway, sadly that isn't at all what God has said in His Word, the Bible. There are if you like 'terms and conditions' which apply to eternal life too. They are not difficult to understand, or written in legal jargon we can't fathom out – they are simple – let me read you something from the Book of Romans chapter 10 and verses 9, 10 and 11.

Saved from what? From God's judgment on our lives, for ignoring what the conditions are for spending eternity in Heaven with Him. That means we reject God's offer of forgiveness for our sins, and not accepting that Jesus really did die on the cross to take the punishment we deserve as individuals.

You see one day every person who has ever lived will stand before God and account for their lives, and it is at that point we are judged and where we spend eternity will be determined.

Contrary to the belief of many folks today, there most certainly is life after death, because we have inbuilt within us by God, a part that will live forever – our soul! That's the bit of us that can know God here and now in this life and have a real relationship with Him. That is our Assurance of a secure future!

You've probably heard of people that have lost out on many occasions in life because they haven't read the 'small print' – they haven't gone thoroughly through the 'terms and conditions', and sometimes we can have a shock when the time comes to make a claim and we find we aren't entitled to what we thought we were!

Concerning our future – it's all in here for the reading (Hold up Bible) – it may seem like 'small print' to you and a drag to read, but it has a critically important message and the consequences really are a matter of life and death for us.

Are you familiar with God's 'terms and conditions' and His' health and safety' regulations for life down here? Believe me those contained in the Bible are of much more importance, and nothing is meant for our detriment – only our Good.

We really should get to grips with reading what God has to say in this book. You may say "It's too hard to understand", "It seems to contradict itself", "I find it hard to believe everything in it". It won't be any good standing before God one day and saying "I didn't know I had to do that" because you have every opportunity to find out.

Psalm 95 verse 7 says "Today if you hear His voice do not harden your hearts". There are many resources to help you read and understand the Bible, so why not get started and have peace of heart and mind in knowing what God requires of us – you'll feel so much better! Whatever you do don't get caught out by not reading the small print!

The Choice is Yours

Subject: The immense choices we have in life – food, clothes, homes, holidays, cars, jobs etc. There is one choice we must make which is more important than any other in life!

Bible Verses: Joshua 24 verses 3, 5, 7, 8, 10, 11-15.

Outline:

1. List some of the choices we have in life and the variety within each category e.g. Food.

2. Some of the more important choices we make as we grow up: friends, career, partner, where to live, jobs.

3. Choices we make require commitment – we have to do something. Some work out well, others don't.

4. We need to involve God in our choices. He knows us each intimately, and what is best for us.

5. We need to reflect on how God has brought us to today, and remember all His goodness to us. Think of examples.

6. Look at Joshua's reminders to the children of Israel, and his challenge to them to 'choose' who they would serve.

7. We have one vital choice we have to make in life, which will not only impact our lives here, but will determine where we will spend Eternity.

8. Choose Jesus!

Prepared Talk

If you go into any Supermarket today and stand in one of the aisles and look at the shelves around you, there are multiple choices for most items. In fact we are spoilt for choice! If you go out for a cup of coffee, there is a whole list of coffees to choose from. Gone are the days when you went into a coffee shop and ordered just a cup of coffee – no frills or froth!

All through life we have choices. From a very young age we begin to choose. We chose our favourite toys to play with, we chose to obey or disobey what Mum and Dad said to us and took the consequences. As we grew up we chose our friends, our career, the person we loved and wanted to marry, whether and how many children we would have, where we lived, holidays and so on through life.

Choices require commitment – we have to do something about each choice we make. For example for our chosen career we have to get qualified, find a job, go and work at it. In a relationship we choose our friends or mate and build up that relationship by doing things with and for them and actively sharing our lives with them. With our homes – we choose where we want to live, find a house, commit to buying it, move in and build a lifestyle. But every choice we make not only requires commitment, but to each choice there are consequences. Some choices work out well and others don't. If before making a lot of our choices we spent more time thinking it through and considering the consequences, and asking God's help, then we would probably make more wise and right decisions!

Of course to seek God's help in anything means that we actually choose to involve Him in our lives to start with. Sadly these days, many folks think they don't need God and He has become an 'optional extra' for when we run into troubles and difficulties.

We are each made up of three parts – body, mind and spirit (soul). We choose how we care for our bodies – feeding them, clothing them, looking after them. We like to feed and keep our minds healthy too by reading, conversation, social interaction, learning and using our intellect, skills and talents. But when it comes to our soul – the very deepest part of us – the part which relates to our spiritual wellbeing and our relationship with God our Creator and Heavenly Father – very often that's a choice which is way down our list of priorities – yet it is more important than anything else in life.

In the Bible some very important characters made choices which affected others and brought varying consequences, God's people the Israelites were constantly being reminded by their leaders of God's goodness to them and His desire that they should stick to Him and worship Him instead of other false gods. But they had the choice, God never forces Himself on us! Let's have a look at some things they were reminded about through Joshua their leader one day:

God had taken Abraham their Ancestral Father and blessed him with many descendants of whom they were some. He had sent Moses and Aaron to lead them out of Egypt where they were captives. When the Egyptians pursued them God divided the Red Sea and the Israelites crossed safely, then God closed the waters and The Egyptian army were drowned. God had enabled them to win battles against their enemies, and delivered them from curses. He gave them a land of their own with everything already in it – houses, buildings, vineyards and olive groves – all they needed to live.

After reminding them of all God had done for them Joshua said this:

"Now fear the Lord and serve him with all faithfulness, throw away the gods your forefathers worshipped beyond the river and in Egypt and serve the Lord. But if serving the Lord seems undesirable to you, then choose for yourselves this day whom you will serve… But as for me and my household, we will serve the Lord.

God has been equally loving, good, kind and merciful to us. He has given us the freedom to choose in every aspect of our lives. So what has your choice been concerning God?

In Psalm 139, there is a verse which says: "All the days ordained for me were written in your book before one of them came to be" In other words God has planned for every one of us when we should be born and when we will die. We have no say in it. That is a choice He made before we were born! The choice we have, is what to do about Him!

The days we are living in are becoming very difficult, and we are very soon going to be faced with hard choices. As our governments and authorities become more and more anti-God, and laws are introduced which are clearly against God's laws, what will we do when faced with difficult choices?

When Joshua challenged the people of Israel about their choice concerning God, he said "… choose for yourselves **this day** whom you will serve" – he didn't say tomorrow, next week, next year or sometime – he said today! It's a choice we too must make – going to heaven depends on it!

The Bible tells us: "Today, if you hear His voice, do not harden your hearts." See to it that none of you has a sinful unbelieving heart that turns away from the living God" – Serious stuff. But the underlying reason for our needing to make a choice is God's tremendous love for us. He loves us dearly and longs that we will turn to Him and be His friends. Even those of us who have been Christians for many years, may need to re-evaluate our walk with Him. Many folks these days think that because they believe in

God they are going to heaven, but being a true Christian is more than that, it's a deliberate choice we have to make to accept that Jesus died for us personally; ask His forgiveness for our sins, and invite Him to come into our hearts and lives. That's the only way we will be right with God and go to heaven.

Anger and Forgiveness

Subject: Looking at anger and forgiveness and how we deal with both. Why it's so important to forgive.

Bible References: Genesis 50 verses 15-20
Matthew 6 verse 14
Luke 6 verses 27, 28 and 37
Luke 23 verse 34
Ephesians 4 verse 26
Proverbs 10 verse 12

Outline:

1. Give examples of anger we see around today.

2. What is forgiveness and why do we need to forgive?

3. A good example of forgiveness, is Joseph and his brothers in Genesis 50.

4. The Lord's Prayer. What Jesus taught about forgiveness.

5. Are we forgiven by God? Do we think we need to be? Have we asked God to forgive us yet?

6. The Bible's advice is, "Do not let the sun go down on your anger". Put things right.

7. Have you any unresolved issues of anger which need forgiveness?

8. God's love can help us in forgiving those who have caused us pain and anger. Remember Jesus on the cross and His request for God to Forgive those who put Him there!

Prepared Talk:

How many times do we see folks on TV or in the paper, telling their stories of 'something' horrific or sad that has happened to them and they often end up by saying "I will never forgive that person/s etc." Perhaps people whose child or loved one has been harmed or murdered. Sometimes we hear them say they have actually forgiven the perpetrator. However, in the 7/7 bombings in London, a lady Vicar, whose daughter was killed on the underground train, felt she had to give up the Ministry because she couldn't forgive the terrorists.

How many times in our own lives have we had experiences that have left us reeling with shock, hurt, disappointment, anger and frustration and our reaction inwardly has been the same – "How can I ever forgive this or that".

Let's have a look at what forgiveness is; does it matter? Do we have to forgive? How do we deal with things that hurt us? What about blame?

When things go wrong it seems we always need someone or something to blame. Somehow it makes us feel better when we can transfer our anger and frustration by blaming someone or something, and that person or situation becomes the object of unforgiveness.

To start with, forgiveness means to cease or stop feeling angry or bitter towards someone or about something. Does it matter whether we forgive? Yes it does. Unforgiveness has a negative and damaging effect on us. It breeds bitterness, anger, hatred. It spoils relationships between people, it destroys trust and tears people apart. All of those things can cause stress, anxiety, and literal physical sickness too. The Bible actually says that "A heart at peace gives life to the body but envy rots the bones" – it's not just envy that can damage our wellbeing either! You probably know from personal experience how unforgiveness can make you feel – whether you have or haven't done anything wrong; it damages both the person who refuses to forgive and the 'unforgiven' one.

So do we have to forgive – yes – why? – because God says so in the Bible – which is our manual for life. There are many references to forgiveness in the Bible, and the greatest act of forgiveness ever was when Jesus died on the cross – and that's not fiction – it actually happened; so that you and I could be forgiven for our sins. Now however great or small you think our sins or wrong acts may be, we all do wrong – all the time – and need forgiveness by God because that's not the way He meant us to be, but however good we think we are, we don't meet up to God's standards for us.

Who is familiar with the Lord's Prayer? When Jesus was on earth and preached and taught people about His Father God and how they should live, He told them they needed to communicate with God in Prayer. He gave them an example of how they could and should pray – in order of importance, and the second request we should bring to God daily is to ask Him to "forgive us our sins, as we have forgiven those who have sinned against us" He didn't say "forgive us our sins as we should or might forgive those who sin against us" He said "Have forgiven" – past tense. In other words we cannot come to Him and ask forgiveness for our sins when we have not forgiven others first! Let's read what He said about that in Matthew Chapter 6 verse 14.

So does it matter whether I'm forgiven by God? Yes, it really does. If we ignore and reject God's offer of forgiveness for our sins then we don't go to heaven when we die – it's as simple and real as that!

We have no right not to forgive others – however wicked or evil they have been – because God himself forgives the worst criminals, if they turn to Him – sadly many don't, but they will be punished by having to spend eternity in a place that doesn't bear thinking about – and that too is very real!

Let me ask you this question – Are you forgiven by God? Have you actually asked Him? Have you forgiven – I mean really forgiven those who have wronged you or harmed those you know and love? If not, then perhaps now is the time. The Bible is full of sound advice and one very good piece is "Do not let the sun go down while you are still angry". Why not? Because some anger is sinful and in that situation we are not right with God unless we've asked for His forgiveness over our anger and other things which we know are not right. And who knows whether we will see another day – we can't take life for granted!

Have you got any 'unforgiven' or unresolved situations in your life – even right back to your childhood? Don't let it go on another minute, sort it out – you'll feel a different person and a weight lifted from your heart and mind. You will please the Lord and know forgiveness yourself! It's really worth it!

I leave you with a verse from Proverbs 10 verse 12: "Hatred stirs up dissension, but love covers over all wrongs."

How can we truly forgive? – by allowing God's love to work through us towards those who hurt us. It really works!

Being Alone and Loneliness

Subject: The realities of loneliness and the 'pros and cons' of being alone. How God will help us through these times, as He is always with us!

Bible Verses: Psalm 139 verses 1-18

Psalm 23 verse 2

Outline:

1. Ask the question "How many of you live alone?"

2. Explain the difference between being 'Alone' and 'Loneliness'

3. Go through reasons for feelings of loneliness which many will identify with.

4. Give a personal example of feeling lonely.

5. Things we can do to overcome loneliness.

6. Being alone has positive aspects – time to talk with God, read the Bible, peace and quietness, enjoy hour hobbies, rest, etc.

7. Explain that we are never ever really alone – God is alongside us – Psalm 139.

8. Sometimes a period alone may be necessary for God to show us something we may not see in the middle of all that goes on in our lives!

Prepared Talk:

Alone is rather a sad word really – the dictionary gives its meanings as "having no one else present", "on one's own", "companionless", "lonely".

The word can ignite all sorts of emotions in us – feelings of sadness, rejection, depression, fear even.

On the other hand being alone sometimes can have great benefits. Peace and quietness; we can pursue our interests and hobbies, read a good book, snooze in the armchair, watch what we like on the TV; and eat just what we like too!

But Loneliness is another thing.

How many of you live alone? Do you often feel lonely and isolated?

There are many reasons for feeling lonely at times – the loss of a spouse or very dear friend, even the loss of a pet, loss of mobility, bad relationship, living in a different town or country, sickness, deafness, blindness.

It is often said that you can actually experience a feeling of desperate loneliness in a crowded room, or even out shopping with lots of folks around. So why do we suffer from this awful 'emotion'. I say emotion because loneliness is a feeling – or an emotional reaction or state. The dictionary describes loneliness as 'sad at being without friends or company'.

The feeling of loneliness comes about through our circumstances, often beyond our control, but it is something we can change. The feelings associated with loneliness are emptiness, isolation, rejection, frustration, sadness, sorrow (as we dwell on the past) and worry (as we think about the future alone).

The reality of loneliness – and it is a very real thing, is that we have no-one to talk to if we live alone; no one to care for; no one to come home to when we go out; nothing to get up for – loss or purpose. It often involves a change of lifestyle and major adjustment; because of a home move; no one to go on holiday with; loss of freedom if we have to go into care; feeling trapped if not able to drive.

So when these overwhelming feelings of loneliness come into our lives, what can we do about them, both for ourselves and others?

Whatever our situation – we can make an effort to share our life with others. Not all the time necessarily, but occasionally by inviting someone round for a cup of tea or lunch. It doesn't cost a lot, we don't have to be brilliant cooks, or live in a palace, but inviting someone to visit works two ways, they will feel wanted and you will feel needed!

However, there is a very positive aspect to being alone, whether long or short term, forced upon us or chosen. There is much in the Bible about being alone and it is actually recommended for us at times.

Of course, as believers, we know that we are never <u>ever</u> actually alone. The Lord is always with us, but the thing that gets us is 'loneliness'!

It is something we have to come to terms with, and accept that being alone for whatever reason is a **fact**, but loneliness is a **'feeling'** and there is a big difference! We may not be able to change the fact but we can deal with the feelings – because feelings come and go!

God made us social beings, and much of the Bible talks about our necessary interaction with, and love and care for each other.

We are also reminded that we are part of a body, we are designed to live and function in dependence on one another.

But, there are times when it's good and right to be alone. It's during those times that we can communicate with the Lord, read His Word, and listen to what He will say to us. Many of you who live alone may not like being in that situation, but whatever your personal circumstances, the Bible tells us we need to spend time alone with God. You may be thinking, well, I've got all the time in the world because I live alone; but how much of your time is set aside to spend with the Lord – It's at those times that we can become very aware that we are not really alone, the Lord is near, and we can feel His presence with us. Read Psalm 139 verses 1-18.

All through the Bible we read of those who were 'alone' with God for varying reasons and lengths of time, but the effect it had on them was staggering. Jesus Himself set the example of being alone with His Father. If Jesus needed to, then how much more do we! Let's have a look at some of those folks in the Bible and how being alone benefited them.

Joshua – After the death of Moses, Joshua was alone and the Lord told him that he would be the one to lead the Israelites to the promised land. A huge responsibility and an honour. But God reassured him by saying, "As I was with Moses, so I will be with you, I will never leave you or forsake you" – that applies to us today. In whatever situation we find ourselves we are never alone!

Gideon – was alone threshing wheat when he was commissioned to save Israel. Again the Lord said "I will be with you" and we know the way the Lord helped Gideon save the Israelites!

Moses – was on his own with a flock of sheep when God spoke to him from the burning bush and told him to go to Pharaoh and take the Israelites out of Egypt. Again God said "I will be with you" a terrifying moment for Moses, but Pharaoh let them go!

John the Baptist – was alone in the wilderness but God was with him as he prepared the way for Jesus.

John – was banished to and totally alone on the island of Patmos when the Revelation was given to Him of what is to come. He was terrified but was reassured and told not to be afraid.

It has been said that "If the Lord's people spent more time alone with Him, we would have spiritual giants again". We have just lost one of those, and a light has gone out in our world – Billy Graham.

Although we may live alone and often feel lonely, the fact is that we are not alone when we belong to the Lord, and He longs that we would spend more time talking to Him and reading His word.

If, when the feelings of loneliness creep in, we would simply remember the promises of the Lord, that we are never alone and that these are only feelings and they will pass as quickly as they came, then we will be able to experience the hope and peace that can flood our hearts and minds, and we can go about our daily lives without being overwhelmed by these emotions.

The Lord is waiting for us to lift our eyes and hearts to Him when we feel lonely, and He will comfort and lift our spirit as we trust Him. Psalm 23 verse 2 says He leads us beside quiet waters and He restores our soul.

He is closer than we think, and always by our side!

Who do you think you are?

Subject: Many today are looking for their identity and want to know their background.
Our true identity as Christians and part of God's family is found in Jesus Christ.

Bible References: John 15 verse 16

Colossians 3 verse 12

2 Corinthians 5 verse 17 & 20

Philippians 3 verse 20

Outline:

1. Today many people are searching their family history to find their identity.

2. Identity is important to us – knowing who we are and where we came from.

3. We may not like what we find, but one thing is sure – we have special identity in God when we belong to His family.

4. We are Chosen, Dearly Loved, Justified (not condemned), A New Creation, Fellow Workers with Him, Ambassadors, Heirs (His children) and we have Citizenship in Heaven!

5. That is all the identity we will ever need!

Prepared Talk

You have probably seen or know of a current programme on TV called 'Who do you think you are'. A team of people research your family background and come up with all kinds of information and surprises they have found out about your family history – not always good either! Usually the programme is focused on a celebrity or well-known person.

Today there seems to be an interest and desire for folks to know where they've come from and who they are, and there are many reasons for that. Some may not have known one or both their parents, as they were adopted when young; some were put into care and have no idea of their background and roots. Many people are feeling insecure, and are looking for some sense of belonging. Is it surprising they feel this way in a world where many are not even sure what gender they are? Our children are being taught things which are totally against God's instructions, and they are confused, some at having two mothers or two fathers!

Even some churches have lost their identity! Sadly in their efforts to become 'user friendly' and politically correct they seem to have lost sight of their real purpose, to preach the Gospel of the Lord Jesus – Some are even embracing things which God forbids! We are clearly told not to conform to this world. The Christian Church needs to stand out and maintain its spiritual identity.

Family history though is not what we are going to think about today. It's not about what was or may have been in our backgrounds, but about the here and now and our future!

Our identity is important to us – knowing who we are and where we came from, from a family perspective; but more importantly, we can know who we are in God's eyes, and our identity in Christ – which matters more than anything we can dig up about our family history!

Looking through the Bible there is a significant list of characteristics which identify who we are in Christ Jesus. That is where our true identity lies. Of course we are all from a family and can go back in time to see the family's history, which is interesting and informative, but we cannot change the past whatever we may find out! It's who we are now which is important.

Let's have a look at some of the things which confirm our Identity in the Lord:

We were **CHOSEN** by God. We didn't choose Him, He chose us before time began and although we have freewill to choose or reject His love for us – He knew those who would become His. As we come to Him our identity is revealed, we become 'a chosen people', people belonging to God, so that we can declare the praises of the one who called us out of darkness into His wonderful light!

From a human perspective it's always nice when we know we have been 'chosen' for something – to receive an award; to be invited to a Wedding; to be offered a position. It makes us feel special and valued. How amazing it is to actually be chosen by God!

We are **DEARLY LOVED** – Colossians 3 verse 12 says this "therefore as God's chosen people, Holy and dearly loved…" How important it is for us in everyday life to know and feel that we are loved by those around us, but to be told that we are dearly loved by God is something which should make us feel very special indeed.

When we respond to God's love and turn to Him in repentance and ask for forgiveness, we are **JUSTIFIED** by faith – I love the way we sometimes hear justification described – it's <u>just as if I'd</u> never sinned! Because of what Jesus did on the cross for us in taking the punishment for our sins on Himself, we are no longer condemned! That surely must humble us.

We can all think of instances in life when we have been accused of doing or saying something wrong and someone has stepped in and spoken on our behalf and we've been vindicated – it's a lovely feeling to have that burden lifted and know you are absolved from blame, you are no longer held responsible – your slate is clean! That's how we are in Christ free from condemnation!

We are a **NEW CREATION** – we are made new in Christ so that we can carry out the good works prepared for us to do before the foundation of the world! That's mind blowing! Way back then God had plans and work set aside for us. We become His **FELLOW WORKERS** – what an honour! Colossians 3 v 12 cont'd.

God has put us in a church – the body of Christ – and it is there that we have a particular function as part of the body and we must do what we feel He has given us to do. It's such a joy and privilege to share what we've learned about Him. 2 Corinthians 5 verse 17-20 says we are His **AMBASSADORS**!

On an individual level we are His **CHILDREN**, His **HEIRS** – we have been sealed with the Holy Spirit as a guarantee.

Our bodies are a temple – the place where God's Holy Spirit dwells. We are not our own – how sobering is that. Surely in view of such a position how should we really be living!

Lastly, Our future and **CITIZENSHIP** is in heaven. Philippians 3 verse 20 says: If only we could grasp what that means for us. We have become very settled in this life and probably spend little time thinking about what is in store for us in the future. As things get more difficult in this world, it is really reassuring to know who and what we really are when we become the Lord's and that our future is secure and bright.

In Christ I am:

Chosen

A New Creation

Not Condemned

Dearly Loved

His Fellow Worker

His Ambassador

Confident – not Afraid

A Citizen of Heaven

Do you have a better idea of who you really are now?

Why does God allow Suffering?

Subject: A question in everyone's mind at some point In life. The reasons are many and complex and we don't have a complete and definitive answer, but the more we learn about God, and accept that He is in complete control, we can see this issue In a different light.

Bible Verses: Job Chapter 1

Outline:

1. We are living in a difficult and troubled world.

2. Many have chosen to deny God's existence because they can't reconcile a 'God of Love' with so much misery.

3. Others believe in an all-wise, all-powerful God, who sometimes uses evil and brings good.

4. When we look at who God is; His dealings with mankind through the ages, we can begin to see there is a much greater plan. Faith in His infinite wisdom is the key.

5. Some possible reasons God allows suffering may be:

   To get our attention
   To guide us
   To shape us
   To bring us together

6. Much of the suffering in the world sadly is due to sin, and the state of peoples' hearts, and part of the answer lies with people realising they need to turn back to God.

7. Our world would be a very different place if we allowed God into our lives and world.

8. The Bible tells us that one day there will be a new Heaven and a new Earth, where there will be no suffering, sadness or tears; no sickness or dying. God Himself will dwell with men and women that have turned back to Him for forgiveness.

Prepared Talk

We are living in a difficult world, and life can be tough. There are many things we don't understand – especially suffering.

There are many questions in our minds which we want answers to, such as 'why do bad things happen to good people, and vice versa?

It would seem to make sense to most people, that a terrorist would be killed by his own bomb; a dangerous reckless driver would end up having a serious accident; or a chain-smoker would get lung cancer, but what about all the innocent men women and children who are killed by terrorists, the driver who suffers unspeakable injuries because of a drunk driver who crosses the centre line and hits them; and the 2 year old who has leukemia?

We don't have a complete answer as to why God allows suffering and the reasons are many and complex. We also have no right to demand that we should understand.

In the Bible one of the most classic examples of suffering was Job. He realised that although many awful things were happening to him, he had no right to demand an answer from God as to why.

At this point I think we need to remind ourselves of who God is!

Many questions are asked on a daily basis in our world of pain – where is God in all of this? If He's good and compassionate why are there so many tragedies? Has He lost control of His world? If not what is He trying to do to you and me and to others when things go horribly wrong?

Many people have chosen to deny God's existence because they can't imagine a God who would allow so much misery. Some think He might love us, but He has lost control of this rebellious planet. Others cling to belief in an all-wise, all-powerful, loving God who somehow uses evil for good!

When we study the Bible, we find it tells us of a God who can do anything He chooses to do. Sometimes He performs miracles on behalf of His people, other times He has chosen not to stop tragedy. What we have to remember is that He is so much bigger, sees everything, knows everything and has done, from before time as we know it, and will into eternity.

Although He is intimately involved in our lives, sometimes He appears to be deaf to our cries for help. In the Bible He assures us that He controls ALL that happens in this world and the heavens and infinity that surround it, but sometimes allows us to be the targets of evil people, bad genes, dangerous illnesses or natural disasters. To us it's a puzzle – suffering. BUT God has given us enough information to help us trust Him, even when we don't know everything or the reasons why.

There are some things that may give us basic answers as to 'why' God allows pain and suffering:

To get our Attention

As much as we hate pain or discomfort, it is there for a purpose. In the physical sense pain alerts us to something that is wrong.

Pain is a symptom which warns us that part of our body is in danger or under attack.

Something's wrong with the world – the state of our world right now tells us that something is very wrong. The difficulties we experience and the distress we see in others shows us that suffering does not discriminate because of race, social status, religion or even morality; it can seem cruel, random, purposeless, grotesque and out of control at times. The seeming unfairness of it all has come close to each of us.

It seems many people suffer through no fault of their own – an accident, a birth defect, a genetic disorder, abuse, chronic pain, troubles with children, severe illness, the death of a partner or child, broken relationships, natural disasters – the list is endless and it doesn't seem fair. Couldn't God have created a world where nothing would ever go wrong? He could have but He didn't. He gave us the gift of human freedom, the ability to choose, and that carried the risk of us making wrong choices.

Disease, Disaster and corruption are symptoms of a deep problem – the human race has rebelled against their Creator. All the sorrow, grief and pain are reminders of the way humans are and that the world is not the way God created it to be.

The first and most basic answer to the problem of the existence of suffering, is that it is a direct result of sin coming into the world. Often our troubles may be merely the side effects of living in a fallen world, and may be through no direct fault of our own.

Something's wrong with us – We can be targets of cruel acts by people or from Satan's demons. Both fallen human beings and fallen spirits have the capacity to cause damage to themselves and others.

Suffering caused by people – People make bad choices in life and they often affect others. The hurt that others inflict on us may be due to their selfishness, or we may be persecuted because of our faith. Through history, Christians have suffered at the hands of people who rebelled against God.

Suffering caused by Satan and his Demons – The story of Job is a real example of satanic attack. But God allowed it! Job was told to curse God and die by his wife, but Job maintained his integrity even when his life completely fell apart, because God is worth trusting.

In the end, even though Job didn't understand what God was up to, he had reason to believe that God was not being unjust, cruel, sadistic or unfair, because He knew God for who He was and knew that those were not characteristic of God. And in the end because he maintained his trust, God blessed him so much more and he had more given back to him than he'd ever had in the first place.

He said "Shall we indeed accept good from God, and shall we not accept adversity?"

Something's wrong with me – Often when things go wrong in our lives, we immediately assume that God is punishing us because of some sin we've committed. But that's not necessarily true at all. Much of the suffering that comes into our lives is because we live in a broken world inhabited by broken people and satanic spirits.

We do need to deal with the hard fact that some suffering does come as the direct consequence of sin – either because God wants to correct us because He loves us, or of His reaction to rebellion in His world.

If we trust Jesus, we are children of God and part of a family headed by a loving Father, who trains and corrects us. He's not an abusive, sadistic parent who dishes out beatings because He gets pleasure out of it. Jesus said "As many as I love, I rebuke and chasten…"

Most of us would understand that a loving Father would correct us and want us to obey Him.

God also deals with stubborn unbelievers who persist in doing evil, and if they continue to disobey and reject God's love, they can expect to receive His wrath at a future day of judgment and even face the danger of severe judgment now, if God so chooses.

God destroyed decadent humanity before by the flood, and destroyed Sodom and Gomorrah because of their disgusting perverted behaviour, so in some ways is it any surprise that He sometimes allows suffering in the here-and-now, to try and bring people to their senses before they face the wrath of God on judgment day?

Having said all of that, God is loving and just and doesn't want any single person to perish and go to Hell, and will forgive them immediately they turn back to Him.

To Guide us

Sometimes when people suffer, they will turn away from God, blaming the suffering. but sometimes suffering gets the credit for people's lives being turned around, because it helped them to see things more clearly and brought them closer to God.

Suffering can produce a healthy dependence on God.

Suffering has a way of showing us how weak our own resources are. It makes us rethink our priorities, values, goals, the source of real strength and our relationships with other people and with God. Suffering forces us to re-evaluate the direction of our lives.

We can choose to despair by focusing on our problems or we can chose to hope by recognising God's plan for us – Jeremiah 29 verse 11.

Pain of any kind forces us to look beyond our immediate circumstances and makes ask big questions like "Why am I here?", "What's the purpose of my life?". By looking for and finding the answers in the God of the Bible, we will find the ability to endure the worst that life can bring us, because we know that this life is not all there is. When we understand that a sovereign God is in control of all human history and making it into something that will eventually glorify Him, then we can see things in a different way.

Read Romans 8:18. Paul wasn't being dismissive about our troubles and trials but tells us to look at them in the light of Eternity – the bigger picture! Things may be awful for us but Paul said by comparison with the incredible things that await us, even the darkest times will be put in perspective.

Perhaps the most significant illustration we can think about is the day that Jesus hung on the cross. That Friday was anything but a good day, it was a day of intense suffering anguish, darkness and gloom. Jesus felt all alone. God seemed absent and silent and evil seemed to triumph, but then came Sunday – Jesus rose from the grave. That awesome event put Friday in a different light! We too, can look ahead. We can endure our dark 'Fridays' and be able to look on them as good because we know the God of 'Sunday'!

To Shape us

The Apostle Paul suffered a lot of pain in all kinds of ways, and he said this "We also glory in tribulations, knowing that tribulation produces patience, and patience character, and character, hope" Romans 5, 3 & 4.

How can we say that we should rejoice or be happy that we are having to endure some painful things in our lives? Paul was actually telling us that we can be happy about what God can and will do for us and for His glory through our trials. We are to celebrate the end product, rather than the painful process!

How have you responded to the difficulties of life? Have you become bitter or better? Have you grown in your faith or have you turned away from God. Have you let them shape you and make you more like Jesus?

God is using all of life to develop us and build our characters and make us more like Jesus, to further His eternal plan. He wants to use us to help others and others to help us.

To Unite us

Pain and suffering of any kind shows us that we need each other. In our Church fellowships we can share each other's burdens when things go wrong, and it draws us together as we support one another.

As we experience the comfort God can give in difficult situations, we can encourage those going through similar things.

God uses suffering to bring our attention to the problem of sin. He uses difficulties to guide us to Him, and He even uses problems to make us more like Jesus!

It's the love of God through us which makes a difference to others' suffering. It's the love and peace of God within us personally which enables us to get through our own suffering.

Heaven

Subject: What can we know about Heaven?

Does it really exist?

What will it be like?

Will we all go there when we die?

Bible Verses: Exodus 20 verse 22

1 Kings 8 verse 30

Isaiah 66 verse 1

John 14 verses 2 & 3

Philippians 3 verse 20

Outline:

1. Talk about what we would consider 'paradise' to be like.

2. Will we all go there when we die? (Explain John 14 verse 4)

3. What will Heaven be like? Free from all that is bad!

4. Our earthly home is temporary – heaven will be our home for ever (John 14 verses 2 & 3

5. We need to think now about Heaven – will it be our final destination? There are 2 options!

6. Explain the only way we can be sure of going to Heaven when we die.

Prepared Talk

Have you ever been on a holiday or visited somewhere and thought 'this is paradise' – it's beautiful, warm, quiet and I'm away from all the hassle and troubles of daily life? As much as we may enjoy our lives, there are always time of hardship and difficulty, be it money worries, health problems, family issues – whatever, and we long to get away for a while just to relax and have a change.

One of the topics of conversation often raised by folks today is Heaven – is there such a place? The answer is absolutely Yes! Some people don't like to talk about Heaven as they think it means thinking about death, but that's not so, it's thinking about something good, exciting and full of hope!

Where is Heaven? What's it all about? What's it like? Will we all go there when we die? Will we see those we've loved who have died?

In the Bible there are over 600 references to Heaven. So what can we know about it?

Firstly, it's the place where God dwells. The Bible tells us that. It doesn't mean of course that if God is in Heaven, He isn't with us on earth. His presence is everywhere, but His dwelling place is in Heaven.

There are many references to Heaven in the Bible. We can't pinpoint heaven as a geographical place, or find a reference for it on our SatNav's, but the Bible simply tells us that Heaven is where God dwells. We accept that as a fact of our faith. Faith of course is the assurance of things hoped for and the conviction of things not seen! God has promised that He is there, He does hear us when we pray, and there is a home there for us with Him when we die – it's all in here (Hold up Bible).

God is King of the universe He created, and the Bible speaks of His throne being in Heaven. It's from that throne in Heaven that He rules over the affairs of men. He may permit evil men and women to have their day, but he has not lost control of the world, not for one second. God is still in command. It's a lovely thought to know that Heaven is the centre or Headquarters of God's administration and authority – His government if you like.

The Bible also tells us that it's from His throne in Heaven that God accepts our worship and hears our prayers. God has promised to listen to the prayers of His people and He will hear and respond. We are told in Hebrews that there are an innumerable company of angels who are in heaven around God's throne, and there they receive their orders and are continually going back and forth from heaven to earth obeying His instructions concerning us! How amazing is that.

Heaven of course is also our final home. It's the place where His people, those who have given their lives to Jesus, will go after this life is over. When we die as Christians, our soul immediately goes into the presence of Jesus. Our soul is separated from our body and we enter our eternal home. Not everyone will enjoy the glory and the wonders of heaven. There is one condition which must be met –faith in God's Son the Lord Jesus.

Most people would agree with the saying 'Home is where your heart is'. It's the place where we can be ourselves, a place of safety, warmth and comfort. Deep down, home is the best place to be on earth – it's where we belong. There's always something so special about coming home, when we've been away for a while. But one day, we will go to our Heavenly Father's home – heaven. It will be far better than any 'home' we've ever had here on earth!

We all need to see our lives here as being temporary. Some folks are here for only a short time, others are given many more years – the average being 70 according to the Bible!

There was a lovely old song which Jim Reeves, a Country Singer used to sing and the words went like this: "This world is not my home, I'm just a-passing through, My treasures are laid up, somewhere beyond the blue. The angels beckon me, from heaven's open door, and I can't feel at home in this world anymore."

Have you ever lived in temporary accommodation? It's not the same as a permanent home is it? Maybe we should all be thinking a little more about our long-term future – Eternity. We all like to make plans for the future. We plan for our families, their education, their weddings, our grandchildren. We plan for our retirement, we make our Wills to care for our family's future, and that's about as far ahead as we think – why?

The most important thing we can ever plan for is the end of this life and the beginning of the next – that may sound odd, but we were only ever meant to be here for a period of time. God has already recorded the precise length of our lives here, before we were even born. How amazing is that! Our whole life planned by God!

What plans have you made for your future? Where will you spend Eternity. Will it be in Heaven with the Lord, or will it be in the only other alterative – Hell. That may sound very black and white, but that's how it really is. There's no in between. It's what God has said and it cannot be changed. People don't want to talk about it, but it's something we should understand and an issue we must deal with here and now.

Who, in their right mind would think about risking spending eternity away from God?

Are we certain we are going to heaven? Life after death will be as real as life is here – only a million times better in heaven! We need to get enthusiastic and excited. It will be a wonderful place!

Love One Another

Subject: None of us like to think we are talked about behind our back, or have been wrongly accused. The Bible has a lot to say about Gossip and Judging others. This talk encourages us to think before we speak!

Bible Verses: John 13 verse 34
Proverbs 11 verse 13
Proverbs 16 verse 28
Matthew 7 verse 1
James 4 verse 17
Luke 12 verse 3

Outline:

1. Most of us will have had something unkind or untrue said about us behind our back and it hurts!

2. Jesus knew what it was like to be ridiculed, lied about and falsely accused, leading up to His crucifixion.

3. What we say can make or break someone's opinion of another person, so we need to think about how it makes us look, when we gossip or judge others!

4. Talk about gossip – using verses from Proverbs. We all do it, but it is a sin!

   Read out James 4 verse 17.

5. The Bible warns about gossip and innuendo!
   Read Luke 12 verse 3.

Prepared Talk

Have you ever had someone say something about you behind your back that has really upset you and hurt you, because it wasn't true?

For that matter have you also had someone say something unkind about you to your face?

It's very likely that most of us have experienced both of these, and they really hurt don't they!

There is nothing worse than having someone accuse you of something that is totally untrue and you know you're not guilty of. Many, many people all over the world on a bigger scale have been accused and punished even, for something they've never said or done and today there are folks locked up in prisons who are totally innocent.

Jesus Himself knew what it was like to be ridiculed, lied about and falsely accused. Whilst He was here on earth preaching and teaching people about His Father and how they should live their lives to please God, He gave us instructions about how we should treat others. The Bible is very clear about two things in particular that we are all guilty of at times, and if we profess to be Christians, we must absolutely not do. Even if we are not Christians yet, but go to Church or attend meetings like this, people identify us with the Church and God, and are always watching how we behave!

Things we say and do, can make or break someone's opinion of what a true Christian is or should be, and we will have to answer to God for our behaviour if it brings His Church into disrepute. So let's have a look at how important these two things are.

Can anyone tell me the second most important commandment that Jesus gave to people when He was talking to them about relationships?

Love one another ! If we are to obey that commandment as we should obey them all, these are two things we must avoid:

Gossip! What me gossip you say! Yes, because we all do it, sometimes without even realising. So what is Gossip? It's defined in the Bible as "one who reveals secrets, someone who goes about telling tales on others, and someone who is a scandal-monger" A scandal-monger is someone who stirs up public anger towards another by spreading rumours or malicious gossip – basically unkind and untrue things about them.

When we gossip about others, we subconsciously have the aim of 'bigging' ourselves up by making others look bad! Gossips tell about the faults or failings of others or reveal embarrassing or shameful things about them without their knowledge. Even if we mean no harm, it's still gossip!

There are some surprising things in the Bible about gossip, as it is a serious sin! Did you ever think that gossip is a sin?

In the Bible a group who were known for indulging in gossip were widows. The Apostle Paul in the Bible cautions widows against entertaining the habit of gossip. He said they were "gossips and busybodies, saying things they ought not to". Because women tend to spend a lot of time in each other's homes and company they hear and observe situations which can become distorted especially when repeated over and over. He said that widows often had more time on their hands and consequently would be prone to gossip!

Of course, women are certainly not the only ones who gossip. Anyone can gossip simply by repeating something heard in confidence. There's a lot in the book of Proverbs about gossip and the dangers and potential hurt it causes. It says "A gossip betrays a confidence, but a trustworthy man keeps a secret". It also says a Gossip can separate close friends. Many a good friendship has been ruined over a misunderstanding that started with gossip. Those who gossip do nothing but stir up trouble and cause anger and bitterness and pain among friends. Usually when they are confronted they deny it and make excuses rather than admit that they've done wrong. This is all too familiar isn't it because we're all guilty of gossip at times.

So God wants us to guard our tongues and stop the sinful act of gossip. It is difficult not to gossip at times, but if we mean to live the Christian life and be an example to those around us, we need to follow what the Bible teaches. One day, we will all have to answer for the way we have lived our lives here.

The other thing Jesus wanted us not to do is judge others! He said "Do not judge or you too will be judged". Many people use this verse to shut their critics up, and interpret it as "You don't have the right to tell me I'm wrong". By telling us we are not to judge others, doesn't mean that we can't show discernment. He does want us to be able to tell right from wrong, and identify sin for what it is, based on what God says is sinful.

By saying that we shouldn't judge people, Jesus wasn't saying that anything goes!

He gave some clear guidelines as to how we should not judge people:

1. <u>Superficial judgment</u> – in other words don't judge someone by appearances only. Don't jump to conclusions before you know the facts!

2. <u>Hypocritical judgment – </u>Don't judge another for a sin which you yourself commit!

3. <u>Harsh, unforgiving judgment</u> – We should always be gentle towards everyone. If we judge others harshly, and in an unforgiving way, we too will be judged. We must show mercy.

4. <u>Self-righteous judgment</u> – We should never judge with a self-righteous attitude. We are called to be humble because God hates pride, and He knows what's in our heart!

5. <u>Untrue judgment</u> – We are not to tell lies about someone. The Bible warns about bearing false witness (telling lies). Slander no-one!

6. Opposing sin is definitely not wrong, and God has told us clearly what is not right, and things we must not do.

If we profess to be Christians and others hear us gossiping about someone or judging them, we need to remember that God also sees and knows what we do. If we are to obey what Jesus said we should do, and love one another, then we need to treat each other tenderly, with respect, and mercy – just as He has shown us, when we are wrong.

Next time we're tempted to get caught up in gossiping or judging someone, remember this little saying, and it may help you not to do it.

Is it Kind?

Is it True?

Is it Necessary?

What does Christmas mean to you?

Subject: A Christmas talk challenging folks to think more about the true meaning of Christmas, by presenting them with some questions, and interspersing the talk with readings.

Bible References: Matthew 1 verses 18-25

Luke 1 verses 26-38

Luke 2 verses 1-20

Matthew 2 verses 1-23

Outline:

1. Ask questions (see Prepared Talk) and suggest answers.

2. Talk about the prophecies concerning Jesus' birth given many years before.

3. Remind folks of the fact that we readily believe things that are written and recorded in thousands of history books – so why don't we believe the Bible?

4. Put the question – Do you know why Jesus came to earth?

5. Look at the Christmas Story again interspersing with relevant readings, commencing with Matthew 1 verses 18-25 and Luke 1 verses 26-38.

Mary and Elizabeth, and Luke 2 verses 1-20.

6. Caesar Augustus called for a Census. This was part of God's plan to have Mary and Joseph in Bethlehem – the place foretold by the prophet for Jesus' birth.

7. Jesus' birth was surrounded by miraculous happenings:

    Mary pregnant by the Holy Spirit

    Joseph told by an Angel

    Elizabeth pregnant with John the Baptist

    Angels appeared to the Shepherds

    Wise men recognised the special star

    The star moved and led them to Jesus

    Wise men warned in a dream to go back home a different way.

    Joseph told by an Angel in a dream to escape to Egypt

    Joseph again directed to go to Nazareth to live

    Jesus would be known as a 'Nazarene' – foretold by the prophet.

8. Angels – God's Messengers

9. Jesus came once, and the Bible tells us He's coming again. Do you believe it? Are you ready? It's true and could happen at any time!

Prepared Talk

Here we are in December and it's Christmas! So what does Christmas mean to you?

A lot of fuss for just a couple of days?

A lot of expense – a shopping frenzy?

A happy time to spend with family and friends?

Christmas lunches, coffee mornings, parties?

The end of another year – perhaps a difficult one and you're glad it's nearly gone?

Another year gone – another year older?

Are you looking forward to a new year?

Do you really enjoy all that goes with the Christmas Season?

What is good about Christmas to you?

What is bad about it for you?

Let me ask you this – do you really know and understand what it's all about? Do you actually believe what it's all about? If you do then how has it affected your life? Does it matter? How many of you could sit down and tell someone the whole of the Christmas Story and what it means?

The birth of Jesus was foretold and written down as much as 1000 years before He was born! In the Old Testament of the Bible we are told which tribe Jesus would come from even, which family He would be born into; where He would be born; the miracles surrounding His birth; the gifts He would be given etc. All of this came true later on and has been recorded for us in this book. So why don't we attach more importance to it and believe it? So few people these days do.

We would never question what is written and recorded in our libraries packed full of history books, so why don't we believe the Bible? That's a big question.

The most important question for any of us to answer today is do you know why Jesus came to earth?

We all enjoy singing the lovely carols and listening to the readings about Christmas but I wonder how much we think during this time about what it all means.

Let's have a fresh look at the Christmas Story to remind us of what it really is all about.

It all began like this…

Reading: *Matthew 1 verses 18-25*

                            Luke 1 verse 26-38

Mary found it quite hard to believe what was happening to her, but God sent her to a relative who was much older, and there Mary found out that her relative also had experienced a miracle from God! An angel reminded her that nothing was impossible with God! And do you know what – He's still the same God today and still performs miracles in people's lives.

One thing we all need to do is remember who God is and how powerful He is.

Mary stayed with her relative Elizabeth for 3 months, which probably helped avoid any unkind gossip and ridicule she may have been subjected to at home in Nazareth because she was pregnant before being married. When she returned home it was almost time for her to give birth.

Read Luke 2 verses 1-20

Caesar Augustus, the Roman Emperor at the time, was demanding a census of the whole Roman world. Probably partly due to his pride and wanting to know how big his empire was and how many people he ruled over! So everyone had to go to the town of their birth and register. But this was all part of God's plan to have Mary & Joseph in the right place at the right time to be where He had planned Jesus must be born. Remember hundreds of years before the prophets had foretold that Jesus would be born in Bethlehem!

Matthew 2 verses 1-23

The record of Jesus' birth in the Bible is surrounded by miraculous happenings:

1. Mary became pregnant – the Holy Spirit of God put the child in her womb.

2. Joseph was told by an Angel what was to happen

3. Mary's elderly relative became pregnant and gave birth to John the Baptist.

4. Angels appeared to the shepherds and told them exactly where to find Jesus.

5. The Wise Men recognised the special star God had placed at that time and set off to find and worship Jesus.

6. The Star moved to lead them and stopped over the place where Jesus was!

7. The Wise Men were warned in a dream not to return to Herod.

8. An Angel appeared to Joseph again in a dream and told him to take Mary and Jesus to Egypt to escape Herod.

9. After Herod had died Joseph was told again in a dream to take them to Israel, but Herod's son was in charge, so Joseph was directed again by God to go to Nazareth, where they settled and lived.

Jesus was known as a Nazarene – something else foretold by the prophets hundreds of years beforehand.

Angels – are not a figment of our imagination, but they are supernatural beings which God uses as His messengers and protectors of his people.

Jesus came once. He has promised He is coming back again to sort out this world – do you believe that? Are you ready? The Bible says we won't know when, but gives us indications as to when it may be near – and it is – all the signs are out there in the way the world is going!

The Garden

Subject: Using our love of gardens and gardening to Illustrate the beauty of the natural world.

Three particular gardens are mentioned in The Bible.

Bible Verses: Genesis 2 verse 4 on.

Matthew 26 verse 36

John 19 verse 41

Outline:

1. Talk about our gardens, their importance to us and how things have changed. They are often now made into hardstandings for car parking; but some are still landscaped.

2. The importance of the garden to our wellbeing.

3. There were three particularly important gardens in the Bible.

4 **Eden** – The place where Adam and Eve were put to live by God.

What happened there changed everything when sin came into the world because of their disobedience.

5. **Gethsemane** – the garden where Jesus spent time praying to his Father, and agonised over what was facing Him on our behalf – the Cross.

6. **The Garden Tomb** – where Jesus' body was laid and where God resurrected him to life and He stepped out of the tomb and people saw Him, proving that He was alive!

Prepared Talk

How many of us enjoy gardening? It may be we only have a small garden or no garden at all; but probably at some time in your life you have had your own garden.

A couple of years ago there were many TV and Radio Programmes, books and magazines on Gardens. Everyone was rushing out and having their gardens re-designed and landscaped. It became quite a lucrative business and garden centres sprung up all over the place.

It's easy to get caught up in the gardening trend and become inspired by some of the amazing things they are able to do with areas that look like landfill sites, and some which are very tiny and you can't imagine could be made into something pretty.

It's rather sad that sometimes, what could be a lovely little green oasis, is often turned into a clinical concrete and gravel showpiece. It's a shame to cover the soil, which has so much goodness and potential and replace it with something cold, hard and colourless.

There is something about a garden, that whenever life gets stressful and tedious, as it surely does at times; to go out and 'potter' or just sit under a tree in peace and quiet and talk to the Lord, puts everything in perspective again.

If we consider what is in the garden, irrespective of the time of day, or the season, there is always something to observe and cause us to marvel.

There's the peace and freshness of the early morning, in the spring and summer months; it's quiet and gentle with the dew twinkling on the grass and plants in the early sunshine, and the little birds singing in the trees around. Even on a bright winter morning when the sunshine glistens on the frost or snow it has a special beauty.

There are lovely fragrances from flowers and shrubs which often go unnoticed because we are so busy rushing around that we have no time to "smell the roses" as they say.

If we look upwards when there is a breeze, although unseen, it is evident as it rustles through the leaves and causes the clouds to glide across the sky.

In the middle of the day the warmth and light of the sunshine has caused all the flowers to open and drink in its goodness.

And then of course there's the evening. What a spectacle on a clear starlit night, if we will just step outside the door into the garden and look up. The heavens above us have a whole majesty of their own.

There are trillions of stars and the more you look the more you see. The full moon which sometimes completely lights up the garden is so bright and comforting in the darkness; there are clusters of stars twinkling which are light years away; the milky way, shooting stars, meteorites, comets and so on. There are also other interesting things to see like satellites gliding across the night sky, the occasional view of the Space station way out there beyond our atmosphere where there are actually people working, suspended in space!

It's all quite wonderful. But you can only appreciate it if you go out and spend time looking at it.

No matter what is happening in our lives, be it good or difficult, stepping into a garden puts things into perspective, as there, we are surrounded by the evidence of a wonderful and loving Creator God.

In the Bible we read of several Gardens which were very significant, and where some major events took place.

The first was the Garden of Eden and we are all aware of what happened there – READ Gen 2 verses 4-10 & 15. God had given the very first person He had created a beautiful and special place to live. He was to work and take care of the garden. God talked with Adam in that Garden.

Sadly though, it was there that the fall of man occurred through disobedience, and because of that Adam and Eve were banished from that lovely place.

Another important Garden in the Bible was the Garden of Gethsemane. It was the place that Jesus went to pray as He was approaching the completion of His work on earth and had to face the cross. It was in that Garden, late in the day that Jesus agonized over what He was facing. It was a place of quiet and tranquillity where He could be alone to talk with His Father.

There was of course another garden mentioned in the Bible of significance. It was the place where the tomb was that Jesus was laid after his death.

It was from that Garden tomb that Jesus stepped early on the morning of His resurrection that first Easter Day. What a morning in that Garden!

Gardens are very special places. It is in a garden that we can witness the miracles of new life, and they hold such lessons for us, and can bring peace and calm into our troubled lives and help us think clearly once more.

Whether you have your own garden or go to a park or a public garden somewhere, remember all that you observe is the handiwork of a wonderful Creator and Loving Heavenly Father who deserves our hearts and our praise.

So in the spring, as you observe the new life emerging, remember that we too can have 'new life' and hope through Jesus, if we will just take time to stop and reflect on who He is and what He has done for each of us as individuals.

A Woman of Faith

(A talk for Mother's Day)

Subject: Talk based on the Wife of Noble Character in Proverbs 31. She has a long list of qualities.

     The most important aspect, although not mentioned, is her faith – without which she probably could not achieve all the rest!

Bible Verses: Proverbs 31

     Hebrews 11 verse 6

Outline:

1. Talk about the trials and testings we encounter in daily life.

2. Look at the meaning of 'Faith' in all kinds of things.

3. From documented evidence and historical facts, we can know that God can be trusted.

4. The Bible tells us that anyone who puts their faith in God "will never be put to shame" (let down!)

5. Faith involves attitude and actions!

6. A mother's faith will have a huge impact on her family.

7. Go through the attributes of a Godly Wife and Mother.

Prepared Talk

Sometimes it seems as though our faith is really tested! It's usually when things go wrong, or we are under extreme pressure.

Let's look at the meaning of FAITH – the Oxford Dictionary says "complete trust or confidence" – but that in itself doesn't mean much – complete trust or confidence has to be IN something or someone. Many would say "in my own abilities to handle life", some would say "in my religious beliefs", I would prefer to say "in God"!

We place our trust and confidence in many things in life – in our parents when we're children, our teachers at school, our friends, our husbands, our jobs, our wealth, our health and so forth, but every one of those without exception can fail us at a moment's notice – we've probably all experienced that, so where do we turn. Well of course I'm going to say To God – but why should we? Because God can be trusted!

You then ask well HOW do you know, give me some proof! Many of us will know that each time we have put our faith totally in God because there has been no other alternative but to do that – He has never failed us. (Give personal examples of times you have had to trust God, and how He has helped you.)

If we dare to put our Faith in God He will NEVER fail us and we will never look stupid – the Bible says that anyone who believes and trusts in the Lord Jesus will be saved (from an eternity apart from God) and will never be put to shame – in other words God will be on your side!

Many people laugh and mock simple faith, yet that is precisely what God requires of us. We don't have to be great philosophers or thinkers, or extremely clever people to believe in God, it's a simple case of exercising a childlike trust and accepting that He is who He says He is and He can do what He says He can for us;

and He is with us all the time and loves and cares about our every move. Have you ever watched a Dad playing with his little child and tossing it up into the air and catching it again, and the child is laughing and pleading for more? Or a child up a tree or on a wall and the Father tells it to jump and he will catch it? The child without hesitation throws itself into its Father's arms because it KNOWS the Father will not let it fall or get hurt – that is TRUST!

Now Faith is not just about trusting. It's about acting on what we believe also. The Bible says Faith without works is dead. In other words, how will anyone know about your faith if you don't show you have it? A woman's faith can have a huge impact on those around her, and the Bible makes mention of several women's faith.

There was a young preacher who worked with the Apostle Paul, called Timothy, and Timothy had been greatly influenced in his young life by the faith of his Grandmother Lois, and his mother Eunice.

Faith is shown by our Attitude firstly and then our Actions! Our faith will give rise to our actions.

Faith also has another meaning – it is believing in something we hope for but cannot see. We cannot see God now, but we believe and live in the hope of seeing Him one day face to face. Faith is the foundation of our Christianity.

In Proverbs 31 there are some wonderful verses about a 'Wife of Noble Character' (Read Chapter)

Could you be called a Woman of Faith?

Let's look at the attributes or qualities of a good Wife and Mother, as the Bible describes her:

• She is a careful woman and works eagerly around her home, keeping it clean and up together.

- She is enterprising – in other words she takes care of her family's needs, she doesn't laze around, but is up early preparing for the day (making sandwiches, getting breakfast etc.)

- She is sensible and careful with money, and saves it by buying wisely.

- She is self-sufficient and grows and makes things.

- She looks after herself and so she is fit and able to care for her family.

- She makes sure she has enough of everything in the house, such as food and things we use every day.

- She is 'handy' – she can make things – perhaps by sewing, knitting, mending, crafts etc.

- She is kind to the poor and helps those in need both in the extended family and among her neighbours and friends.

- When the weather is bad she makes sure the family are dressed warmly.

- She also cares about her appearance and is nicely dressed to make her family and her husband proud of her.

- She uses her skills to help provide for her family financially – these days that would probably mean having a job as well.

- She is strong in character and dignified – confident and calm.

- She doesn't worry about the future.

- She is wise in her talk and a good counsellor or listener.

- Her children and her husband respect her and are proud of her.

- Lastly and most important of all, is her Godly character – she is a Christian! She loves God and from that relationship comes the greatest of all qualities any of us can have and aim for, LOVE.

Now that's a tall order! You are probably thinking, "There's no way I could live up to that kind of standard". Of course we couldn't – in our own strength – but we can try with God's help!

How lovely it would be to be a woman so capable and up together! It's something we can all aim for, especially the honour of being highly thought of by our families, and be pleasing to God.

Hope

Subject: Where do we place our hope?
In things, people, achievements, money?

All of these can let us down. There is only one safe place to put our Hope – in God!

Bible Verses: Jeremiah 29 verse 11
Psalm 42 verse 5
Psalm 91

Outline:

1. Give examples of how we use the word 'hope' so often such as "I hope the weather improves"; "I hope everything goes well".

2. If our hope is to be realised – we need Faith! "Faith is being sure of what we hope for".

3. Ask what peoples hopes are today?

4. How can we be sure our hopes will be fulfilled? It depends where we place them! Give examples of some hopes that probably won't be e.g. winning the lottery; wishing ill on someone who has offended us!

5. Give examples of things God recommends we <u>don't</u> put our hope in.

6. We can put our hope in God because He won't let us down. God has never broken a promise.

7. God has given us the ultimate 'hope', a place in heaven when we die, and a new heaven and a new earth where there will be no more suffering or sadness.

Prepared Talk

According to the Oxford dictionary HOPE is a feeling of expectation and desire for something to happen.

I suspect that without realising it, the word hope comes to us many times a day in our thoughts and conversations:

"I hope the weather improves" "I hope I can get everything done" "I hope the bus comes soon" "I hope I'll have enough money" "I hope so and so rings today". We say things like "I hope you have a good trip" "I hope you soon feel better" "I hope things work out for you"…

If our 'hope' is to be realised, then we need faith. The Bible tells us Faith is being sure of what we hope for. Real hope begins when we put our trust in God, because He is the one who makes things happen!

What are your hopes today? Do you hope you won't get sick; do you hope you'll have a long life? Do you hope you'll have enough money to see you through life? Do you hope for good things for your family and friends? Do you hope you'll go to heaven when you die?

Hope is an important word but it's a 'future' word – hope is looking forward in faith and believing that things will work out, that they will be fine' that we will be looked after and we will be protected. So can we really be sure our hopes will be fulfilled? Yes, we can so long as our hopes are in the right things. By that I mean we don't spend lots of our limited income on buying lottery tickets hoping we will win (though many people do that); we don't hope for things like our nasty neighbour getting their come-uppance as we say! God knows our hearts, minds and motives. When we genuinely hope and pray for something good for someone else or ourselves, He knows and in His time and plans, our hopes will be realised.

We are advised in the Bible what not to rely on or put our hope in. Wealth and possessions; power; status; as they cannot be relied on. We shouldn't put our hope in people – they too can let us down badly. The only safe place to put our hope is in God, because when we really believe in Him and trust Him, He gives us the best, and because He really loves us we can have absolute confidence in our hopes being realised. *Read Jeremiah 29 verse 11.*

Even when things don't go the way we hope they will and we get downhearted – we are encouraged to cheer up and 'hope' in God. *Psalm 42 verse 5.*

Our world today is becoming a difficult place, with many bad things happening all around us. Many folks are worried and frightened, I know that, because they ask often, "What's happening to our world"? They feel out of control and it seems nothing can be trusted or relied upon – our Government, our health service, our banks, our privacy is being compromised by computers being hacked; fraudsters are ringing our homes and getting money from us; our fellow countrymen and women are joining terrorist groups, bent on destroying our lifestyle and lives. How often do we hear their friends and neighbours say when interviewed, that they are really very nice people and they had no idea of the evil they were harbouring in their hearts!

Some days looking at the news makes us feel our world is a pretty depressing and hopeless place. Sadly to a degree this is true. People are motoring through life with no real aim other than gratifying themselves and their own desires, and this attitude is leading to murder, fraud, perversion and so on. I have heard it said recently that man's biggest problem today is SELF! So why is our world in the state it is – because we have put God out of it! I believe we cannot ignore it any more. The natural world is suffering – extinction of animals, climate change, global warming, disasters somewhere every week, Tsunamis, earthquakes, volcanoes, storms – it's as though the earth is hurting too. The economic world is collapsing and things seem to be on a downward spiral – Why is this?

God made this world, us and everything in it. WE are ruining it and have chosen to push Him out. Yet He is the only answer. The more we ignore Him and do our own thing, the more dangerous and desperate things are becoming, and people have the audacity to say "Where was God" when the Paris tragedy happened? Well, God has never moved – we have – away from Him! And it's because of the wicked hearts of men and women that many of these tragedies occur. BUT in the middle of all of this depressing stuff, there is certain hope. All we need to do is trust and believe. The Bible tells us this world will come to an end as we know it one day because God will intervene. Jesus is going to return to this earth.

There is a good book on Hope by Billy Graham and he explains that for the Christian, our hope is not in this life, but in the fact that after our physical bodies die, our souls (the real us) live on in a different dimension and that's where God is – Heaven! It doesn't matter how bad things get here (and they will according to the Bible), we have something amazing to look forward to, and have no need to be afraid. He will look after those who trust in Him

Read Psalm 91

What on Earth is happening?

Subject: Changes in our Society and the wider world which are causing concern. Christians have the answer from the Bible as to why some of these things are happening. Our world is really in a sorry state, but Jesus Christ said He would return one day, and He gave us some signs of His near return to look out for. Are we seeing these signs today?

Bible Verses: 2 Timothy 3 verses 1-4

Matthew 24 verses 3-14

Outline:

1. Many people are asking "What on earth is happening to our world?"

2. Talk about changes in human behaviour, and the changes in the natural world we are seeing.

3. When teaching His Disciples, Jesus told them, just before He returned to heaven after His resurrection; that He would be coming back to this world one day, and He gave signs to look out for when that day was getting close.

4. Jesus told parables about how people should be prepared for His return.

5. Are we listening to the warnings, and the consequences of leaving God out of our lives? Jesus' return will take us by surprise if we're not ready.

Prepared Talk:

As we watch the news on TV these days, how do we feel about what we are seeing? Do we feel sad and sorry that there are so many awful things happening? Do we not really take it in, thinking it doesn't affect us? Or do we ask ourselves the question "What on earth is Happening"?

That's a question constantly being asked by people, particularly those who are not regular churchgoers.

We have seen unprecedented changes over the last 10 years in so many ways in our lives:

Our Country has changed a lot. Our society has become fragmented, as it seems people are only interested in themselves – their aims, ambitions, achievements and material wealth. This is leaving thousands very lonely – and all ages too!

Our Health has changed. Although science has found many cures and new medications and it's said we are likely to live longer, we are finding that there are new diseases and sicknesses – some brought about by unhealthy lifestyles, and heavily polluted towns and cities, and our National Health Service is in crisis.

Our Lifestyles have changed. The food we eat, our working environment, our living standards, and even retirement. Many folks who have worked hard all their lives are finding themselves caring for grandchildren, whilst their parents go out to work to make ends meet. Life is lived in the fast lane and is governed by our diaries!

Technology too, has taken over our lives, and along with that, money and possessions have become 'gods' to many people.

Our Churches have changed too. They are either filled to overflowing, or closing down for lack of numbers. The services are different, the music is different and there are now so many activities all week long, people are suffering from stress and overloading, trying to keep it all going! Sadly, what used to be lively, full churches are becoming supermarkets, social clubs, gyms and mosques. Did you know that in 2012 this country was declared a Secular Country – no longer recognised as a Christian country. How sad is that! What has happened?

Our Laws have changed, and many of them not for the good or betterment of our lives and society! Things which God hates, are now being taken as ok and acceptable and are being promoted as being normal, and the Bible – our handbook for life, given us by God, is considered out of date, archaic and totally irrelevant to our so-called 'progressive' age.

So, we are doing things our way, but this world has a very big surprise coming, and many will rue the day they voted for, or supported things which God says are not acceptable to Him.

There are very many people who are quite frightened and worried by what is happening in the world around us. In just one week – we see terror attacks, murders on the streets of our big cities; people being attacked with deadly nerve agents and acid; paedophiles coming to light; and so it goes, on and on.

In the natural world, we are seeing worrying things happening too – Volcanoes erupting, earthquakes happening, flash floods, thousands of acres of land being destroyed by wildfires, animal habitats being destroyed, the oceans and rivers being polluted by chemicals and plastic waste, weather changes which are causing many other problems for daily living. Day after day we hear of all of these things going on in ever increasing frequency.

So what is the answer to the question – What on earth is happening? Well, according to the Bible, this world as we know it will one day come to an end. God is going to intervene.

Some may ask how we know the Bible is true and to be believed? All of the things which God has said will happen up until today – have happened and millions of people around the world will vouch for the fact that this book is true and totally reliable!

Some of you may attend Church services where certain things are recited before communion is taken, and one thing which is said that you may well have heard or recited yourself many times is –

"Christ has died, Christ is Risen, Christ will come again"

Do you believe what you read in History books? Well this is also a history book (hold up Bible) and contains a record of what has happened in the past. We know Jesus died because people were there and saw it; we know He rose again from the dead because people were there and saw Him… with the nail prints in His hands and His feet from the cross! At Eastertime we celebrate the fact that Jesus is alive, He is for real! There were even witnesses to Him ascending back into heaven after He rose from the dead.

The first two parts of the statement of faith which is read out regularly in church, have actually been fulfilled. So what about the third? Christ will come again.

Before He went to the cross, Jesus told His Disciples that they shouldn't be upset because He was leaving them to go back to heaven, because He was going to 'prepare' a place for all those who believe in Him, and He would come back one day and take them to be with Him.

He told them He didn't know the day that would happen, but His Father, God knew. However, He did say that when the time was getting close there would be certain signs indicating that His return would be soon, and that people should watch and be ready.

For 2000 years Christian men and women have been waiting for Jesus to return, and although there have been some of the signs which could have indicated that He would be soon returning, many more are happening now, and with much more frequency and intensity, and according to many Bible scholars, we really are living in the days just before Jesus comes back!

Let's look at 2 Timothy 3 verses 1-4 – Does that sound like the world we live in today?!

You are probably thinking "what does all this have to do with me?" I just live my quiet life, minding my own business, helping others when I can and doing good works, and when I die I'll go to heaven! Sorted!

But that's not how the Bible says we will get to heaven – being kind and doing good works – if that were the case then Jesus wouldn't have needed to die and take the punishment for our sins on Himself, which is what He did. Every one of us sins, so we all need to be forgiven and made right with God.

Since all the signs are becoming clear that something has to happen very soon to sort the world out, what should we do? We need to be ready. In what way you may ask?

Let's use a simple example:

Someone you love, rings you one day and says I am going to take you on that trip you've always wanted to go on, I'm not sure which day I will come, but be ready, with your case packed and we can go immediately.

Would you fold your arms and say "nice gesture, but I'll believe it when it happens" and you don't bother too much about preparing. I'll wait until they come and then throw a few clothes in a case. After a day or two, when you least expect it, they turn up. You are not ready, and they say the plane leaves in half an hour, and there's no time to pack now. You've missed out!

The Bible tells us that 'now' is the time to get right with God. We still have the opportunity. He is loving and patient and doesn't want anyone to miss out on Heaven, but one day it will be too late, whether that's because we die, or Jesus comes suddenly to take those who belong to Him.

One of our biggest problems today is that we don't listen to warnings! Jesus has told us He will come back, and all the indications are that this will be very soon. Are you ready?

If you are not sure, then talk to a Christian friend or Church Leader, who can help you.

Also by 'Ben' Huddleston:

Inspiring Daily Thoughts...

...to encourage, uplift and challenge

Full colour, illustrated, themed, pocket-sized booklets –
each containing 31 inspirational thoughts (one for each day of the
month) and ending with an appropriate bible verse.

To order, or for more information about these booklets
or to invite 'Ben' as a speaker to an event
please contact 'Ben' Huddleston on: *01275 792665*
or email: *benhuddleston@gmx.com*